INSPIRE BODY, MIND, AND SOUL

Inspire Body, Mind, and Soul

365 Days of Inspirations

Powerful, positive words can spur amazing accomplishments.

Karen Ficarelli

Copyright 2017 Karen Ficarelli

All rights reserved. No part of this book may be reproduced or transmitted, in any form or by any means, without written permission of the publisher.

ISBN-13: 9781544240299

ISBN-10: 1544240295

Library of Congress Control Number: 2017903810
CreateSpace Independent Publishing Platform
North Charleston South Carolina

Printed in the USA

For my husband, Richard, and our three sons, Christian, Ricky, and Dante.

Inspire Body, Mind, and Soul

Always be yourself—the real, imperfect, flawed, different, unique, beautiful you. It is way too exhausting trying to fit in or be someone you are not. Your unique kind of magic attracts the people, places, and things that are best suited for you. Be healthy in body, mind, and soul.

Exercise and diet alone will not give you the body that you desire. Your mind and soul must be equally engaged to reach the goals that you set forth. It is important to your overall health that your body, mind, and soul work together in sync to give you the focus, strength, and empowerment you need. When self-esteem and self-worth rise within us, we take action, expecting to succeed.

Karen Ficarelli

One of the greatest gifts you can give yourself is to respect and honor your body, mind, and soul. Work on you, for you. No one can do your push-ups for you, make you eat healthy food, or give you a positive attitude. It is up to you to exercise each day, eat whole foods, stay positive, be grateful, and find motivation and inspiration in healthy relationships and lifestyle.

Great things take time, so be patient with yourself. Growth is a process. Let go of the world's mind-set of instant gratification. If everything we wanted came easily, we would not really value or appreciate it. You are closer than you were yesterday, and that is what truly matters. Stay focused on your journey.

INSPIRE BODY, MIND, AND SOUL

Fitness ignites a fiery passion in the soul. It will make you feel so alive. Building a strong, healthy body will improve your mental focus and give you a sense of confidence that you never felt before. Do not hide from challenges; rush forward to greet them. When you truly believe in yourself, you're invincible.

Faith in the midst of difficulty saves us from the soul-numbing cycle of self-pity. When you take your eyes off your troubles, focus on God, and trust His perfect timing, everything falls into the proper perspective.

Our bodies are capable of anything we challenge them to do. It is our minds we have to convince. Don't stop when it hurts; stop when you are done. What the mind decides, the body will follow.

Put balance back in your life by doing things that make you smile. Personal happiness can only come from the experience of joy. It comes from feeling good on the inside. Each day, set aside time for you. If you love to sing, just sing. If you love to dance, just dance. Do more of what you love today.

INSPIRE BODY, MIND, AND SOUL

Many people believe they will be happy once they arrive at specific goals they set for themselves. Stop waiting to be happy! The secret to enjoying the dance of life is living in the here and now while holding in your heart that dreams do come true. The energy you feel will attract what you desire.

When choosing a workout time, be sure to select the time of day that's right for you. If you make the time convenient for you, you'll be more likely to stick to a regular routine. Remember, consistency is key to any goal we set for ourselves.

Guilt and self-pity are wasted emotions. Worrying will not change anything; it just sucks the good energy out of your body, mind, and soul. Your thoughts and words are like a magnet. You will project the story that you keep telling yourself. Make it worth sharing.

When you think abundance, it means that you focus not on what you don't have but rather on what you do have. Abundant thinkers are optimists; they have a higher threshold for change, they transition easier, and they manage stress more effectively.

Inspire Body, Mind, and Soul

A new day, maybe a new chapter in your life, can be exactly what you need. Why not take a chance? You will never regret trying. Don't allow fear or procrastination to become your habit. There is no better time than now. Allow your spirit to shine as brightly as possible every single day.

Listening, humility, understanding, and empathy are the roads less traveled. Listen and validate others. What they have to say is always important. Practice the golden rule; treat others the same way you want them to treat you.

Be picky about the energy you surround yourself with. Be healthy and aware of where you share your energy and with whom. Trust your intuition and feelings. Your feelings don't lie. Let the things that don't belong in your life fall away. Allow your spirit to shine.

The difference between where you are and where you want to be is how you think. Today make a conscious effort to meditate on thoughts that will serve your highest and best. Let go of limiting beliefs and people and unhealthy habits.

INSPIRE BODY, MIND, AND SOUL

Stretch into the next level with a positive mind-set. Fitness is not only exercise; it encompasses many different things. A complete fit lifestyle includes daily exercise, a nutritious diet, consistent healthy habits, healthy relationships, and most importantly, a strong faith in yourself.

Exercise your body, mind, and soul. Train your mind like a muscle to push yourself to the next level. Willpower wavers, but healthy habits will take you to your desired destination.

Look at your workout like a mental game. Challenge yourself and win. Cheer yourself on to be a champion. It would be a shame to grow old without seeing the strength and beauty that the body is capable of achieving.

You are the only one stopping yourself or allowing yourself to go further than you've ever imagined. Your success depends on a healthy mind-set. Success and failure depend upon your state of mind. Think it and believe it for a healthy body, mind, and soul.

Inspire Body, Mind, and Soul

Be a giver of love today. The best gift you can give comes from the heart. Encouraging words, a handwritten letter, a hug, and a smile have tremendous value. Keep in mind that a sincere compliment is uplifting and can easily alter the attitude of the recipient. Give out into the world what you would want to receive.

Goal setting is thinking about your ideal future and making a plan to turn your vision into reality. When you set goals, you naturally focus on the result, but you gain so much more. By knowing precisely what you want to achieve, you know where to concentrate your efforts.

Let nothing upset you. Let nothing startle you. Let all things pass ever so lightly that don't serve you. Whoever has God lacks nothing. Today, be content knowing and trusting all good will come to you. God whispers: you are worth knowing, you are worth finding, you are worth loving.

It's not easy or natural for some people to give up control to God, but if you want to save yourself time and trouble, let go and let God do all the work. God always has your back, my friends; His ways are higher and much more purposeful than ours. Have faith and peace in your life.

INSPIRE BODY, MIND, AND SOUL

Make a binding contract with yourself, and get serious about your health and fitness. Write down your goals, and set a realistic timeline for success. Writing your goals is the most powerful tool to help you get started and mentally prepared.

Be true to yourself! Embrace individuality, and know that it's okay to be different. No matter how different it feels at times, being unique means you're brave enough to be your true self. That's always a beautiful thing!

To make great gains, be vulnerable, and take a leap of faith. Be open to learning and experiencing something out of your comfort zone. Don't let fear hold you back from enjoying life. Change is good on so many levels. Sometimes you need to jump in the water and get wet. Confidence comes from doing something amazing.

The way you use your time has a major impact on the quality of your health. Take time for the really important things in life. Your exercise and nutrition should be a priority. Spend quality time with the people who love and support you. We all have the same twenty-four hours in a day; use yours wisely because you always have a choice.

INSPIRE BODY, MIND, AND SOUL

Don't be so focused on tomorrow that you fail to make
the most of today. Tomorrow is not guaranteed. Live
in the moment, and make the most of this amazing
opportunity. Each day is a blessing.

Every time you hate on others, gossip, or put yourself
or others down, you are contributing to low energy and
division. Every time you lift others up in prayer, share
kindness, or show love to others, you are creating a path
to unlimited abundance and potential.

You have all the power to create a life you truly love.
Most people have no idea how amazing their bodies,
minds, and souls are designed to feel with whole food,
lots of water, daily exercise, adequate sleep, prayer,
meditation, and gratitude.

Let go of any grievances to make room for a new vision.
You must choose to be self-sustaining, self-directed, and
self-affirming. You are more powerful than anything
anyone can do or say about you. Affirm something
wonderful and true about yourself. Your words are
powerful. Love and believe your daily affirmations. Say
them several times a day. Visualize them coming true.

Drop whatever you're doing, and focus on your meal.
Shut off all gadgets, phones, games, texting, e-mailing,
TV, or books. Eat mindfully and become fully engaged
in your meal, slowing down to enjoy every
bite. Your food will be better digested, and you'll feel
full and satisfied.

Above all, be true to thyself first. Loving others never
means taking responsibility for their happiness and
satisfaction. The moment you take on that responsibility
for another person, you abandon a piece of yourself,
and that is unhealthy. Love never means making
unhealthy demands. Always set healthy boundaries.

Be kind. If you have the power to make someone happy today, do it. So many people are lonely and hurting. Even the smallest acts of kindness can improve a person's day and bring a quiet sense of peace to yours. You will never regret being kind.

Make your fitness fun. There are so many activities to choose from that you can find some that you actually enjoy. Enjoying your workout is the secret to making it a permanent lifestyle change. Be open to adding new activities to keep your mind and body motivated.

INSPIRE BODY, MIND, AND SOUL

Find your true self, and become the best version of you. Being you is more than enough. Stop trying to be like someone else; they are already taken. Find your true self, and be who God made you to be!

The more you let go of people who don't treat you lovingly, the more you will attract and experience what you really want. Often, out of habit, we hold on to exactly what holds us back.

Karen Ficarelli

You may have forgotten that you could do anything you choose to do. You can have the kind of life you desire. Take a look at yourself; analyze your life and your daily habits. Tell the truth about what you see. Now take one step today that brings forth your power and strength and that takes you closer to where you want to be.

If you are persistent, you will get what you want. If you are consistent, you will keep it forever.

INSPIRE BODY, MIND, AND SOUL

Happiness is so much like fitness. It is a conscious act
that must be built upon daily like a muscle. A healthy,
happy lifestyle doesn't just happen—you make it
happen. Happiness is a choice. Share your happiness
with others, and you will attract more of it. You always
get in return what you give out into the world.

Prioritize self-love, today and every day. The most
important relationship you will ever have is the one you
have with yourself. Nurture your way to wholeness.

Challenge yourself, and never underestimate what you are really capable of. You have all the power. Own it. Dig deep and unleash it today, not tomorrow!

Gratitude is healing; it helps us connect to what is really important. Being grateful helps us stay grounded in love. It grows faith. By making a habit of gratitude, you will start to reveal the magnificent miracle that is your life.

Inspire Body, Mind, and Soul

Start thinking, feeling, believing, and acting in love, rather than fear. Your success depends on a healthy mind-set. Success and failure depend upon your internal state and whether it's based in love or fear. You must love and accept yourself. Working from a place of love will always bring beautiful results in your life.

When you find yourself judging others who don't fit your idea of how to think or what to eat, like, or do with their time…stop yourself! Understand that everyone is seeking human acceptance and unconditional love. Combine your humanness with their humanness, and know we are all less than perfect. Our flaws can be as beautiful as our talents. We all have something to gain and learn from each other.

A grateful heart leads to a positive attitude and will always leave you feeling blessed. Every day brings new lessons and new possibilities. A good life doesn't always depend on good circumstances. The good and the bad are both parts of life. The bad is a learning process; you will always surpass it if you trust God. Every promise God has made has been tested and certified as reliable. Trust that everything happens for a reason.

You cannot continue to do something that you know is destructive and expect to live a balanced, healthy lifestyle. Make today the day you take control of every aspect of your life. Remember, you are worthy of greatness.

Friends nourish the soul. Spending time with your friends will improve your health, happiness, and even your life expectancy. Lifetime friendship is medicine for the soul.

If you want to be truly happy in all seasons of your life, cultivate a daily healthy habit of being grateful. Begin each day by counting your blessings. Focus on all that you have, naming all of the people, pets, and precious events that shape your life. The more you focus your thoughts on all you have, the less time you will waste on worrying about the things you don't.

Many people think they cannot control their thoughts. Negative thoughts are like any bad habit that you can change. It takes patience and practice to exchange a bad habit for a good habit. Write down everything you are thankful for. Visualize a scene that makes you happy. Negative thoughts will creep in, but don't fall prey to them. Instead, focus your attention on something that makes you happy. Stand strong against negativity. You have the power to choose your thoughts.

Exercise the habit of excellence. The pursuit of excellence is gratifying and healthy. Don't confuse perfection with excellence. The pursuit of perfection is frustrating, neurotic, and a waste of your time. No one is perfect but all of us can excel. Exhaust all efforts, and go the extra mile in everything you do.

INSPIRE BODY, MIND, AND SOUL

Life has a funny way of teaching us lessons. When there is something we need to learn, something that we need to work on, the same situation will continue to repeat itself until we either learn our lesson or find a healthy way of dealing with that particular issue. Balance, patience, and consistency are always our ultimate goals for living a healthy lifestyle.

Healthy weight loss doesn't happen overnight. Patience, especially with yourself, is key to long-term success. It's important to remember that losing weight takes time and continued effort. If the pounds aren't melting off fast enough, the worst thing you can do is to give up. The secret to weight loss is eating whole plant foods along with daily exercise. Make a healthy lifestyle your daily habit until it's as natural as brushing your teeth. Make it feel good and right for you so you keep doing it! No more stopping and starting over. Just keep going!

See in your mind your perfect picture of health, not someone else's picture. Visualize you; get a clear vision of you at your best. This is your goal: to stay focused, motivated, and inspired. You really got this!

You can't out-train a poor diet. Eighty percent of the fat-loss battle boils down to nutrition. Food is not the enemy; food is the answer. Portion control is key even with healthy foods. Try swapping the traditional three meals a day to five to six small, healthy meals centered on whole foods. You'll never be hungry, and you won't be tempted to overeat.

Inspire Body, Mind, and Soul

Don't let the sun go down without having exercised. We are creatures of habit, so don't give yourself an out. You always have time for a run or walk if you make it a priority. No more excuses. Remember, you only regret the workout you didn't do.

When you look at the glass as always half empty, you close your eyes to the abundance right in front of you. If you have a heart and mind of pessimism, the course of your life will be very different from that of someone with a positive outlook. The bottom line is you alone get to choose; no one else can do this for you.

No one is in charge of your happiness except you. Stop living your life wishing for the perfect weight, mate, family, or career. You have all the power to take the necessary steps for change. Change is needed to better yourself, love yourself, and find your truth.

You can assist humankind by evolving higher thoughts. Prayer and meditation are gifts to all. It's time to become aware of your own personal energy that you send out on a daily basis.

Inspire Body, Mind, and Soul

Embrace life as if you are writing a book. Put a positive spin on each chapter, and make your own happy, healthy ending. Every day is a new opportunity to find joy and happiness.

Trust your vision. Even though hardships may arise, keep your eyes fixed on your goal. Every time you go against that intuitive voice, you are not honoring yourself. Follow your gut instinct, and fight to put your intuition into action. The more you do it, the easier and more second nature it becomes.

Until you give up the idea that happiness is somewhere else, you will never be happy where you are. Open your eyes, your mind, and your heart to the opportunities that surround you. Trust that you are exactly where you need to be on your journey to evolve to your highest and best self.

This is your wake-up call to love and respect yourself. It's your life and your call, and most importantly, the change you desire has to start with you. Become the person you admire. Change your habits and change your life.

Inspire Body, Mind, and Soul

Be happy for and celebrate other people's accomplishments. Reach out and offer help in times of need. Be supportive when others need you. This is how you show your true character. Love is meant to connect you; love is why we are here.

Intention is your most powerful tool. It's a discipline that must be affirmed and carved into your heart to fully enjoy the benefits. What allows the intention to fully manifest is the presence of trust and nonattachment to the outcome.

Never mistake a good thing for an easy thing. What we nurture grows. Being fit and healthy is a discipline and requires a lot of effort.

Life becomes more enjoyable when you accept and surrender. There is so much freedom in letting go of all unanswered questions. Forgive who and what hurt you, and understand what it taught you. Celebrate this amazing journey we call life. It's really as beautiful as you want it to be.

Inspire Body, Mind, and Soul

True friendship is about actions. Friends will fight for you, respect you, include you, encourage you, need you, deserve you, stand by you. Today, celebrate your best friend, and let her or him know how important she or he is to you. Healthy friendships enrich your life and improve your health.

Every moment gives you a new beginning and a new ending. You just have to take it and make the best of it. Spending today complaining about yesterday won't make tomorrow any brighter. Take action, and let what you've learned improve how you live today. Make a change and never look back.

The deepest hunger of the human heart is to feel understood, valued, and respected. Sincere connection to others satisfies that hunger and nourishes the body, mind, and soul.

Finish what you started. Keep building your character, strength, and endurance so you can evolve into the person God has called you to be. We are all susceptible to getting knocked off course.

INSPIRE BODY, MIND, AND SOUL

You will never know your limits until you push past your comfort zone. Don't stop when your body says so; stop when you decide it's done. When exercising, lifting weights, or cross training, do just a little bit more than you think you can. You will experience big changes in your body, mind, and soul. The pursuit of a healthy lifestyle means you are always pushing harder and reaching further.

Rules for today...Give yourself some TLC. Take a nap, meditate, eat whole plant foods that make your body happy, and speak only loving and affirming words about your body, mind, and soul. Nurture yourself as if you're the most important person you know. Connect with yourself on a deeper level, and listen to the beauty of your heart. Be healthy and happy, and feel loved.

The next time you open the refrigerator, take a moment to think about what you are hungry for. Is it really food? Are you using food as a substitute for love, self-esteem, or comfort? You may be trying to feed your emotions. Emotional eating can become unhealthy eating that can feed feelings of guilt. Take charge of your life, and find the peace you seek through spiritual healing, exercise, and the company of loved ones.

When you are truly comfortable with who you are, life is so much more enjoyable. Let go of others' opinions of you, and stop seeking their approval. Let love and peace reside in you. True success is being happy with who you are and accepting all of yourself.

Inspire Body, Mind, and Soul

Surround yourself with friends who support, encourage, and inspire each other. Help others realize their true value, and show your appreciation for their friendship. Always be a confidence builder, offering praise and support to those around you. Be the kind of friend you would want in your life.

Step out of your comfort zone. Is there something you've never tried before? Yoga? Spin? Zumba? Pilates? HIT? Resistance Bands? Kettlebells? Try something new, and keep it fun and challenging. Confuse your mind and your muscles; keep the body guessing, "What's next?" That's how you progress! That's how you'll see change! Have a friend join you and double your pleasure.

Being well and eating well are all about being more aware of your daily choices. Every choice matters. Making the right decisions to achieve a balanced lifestyle is about learning a new life skill. Pay close attention to any behavior you may be allowing that is hurting your progress. Be aware of every choice you make.

Use positive affirmations to raise your energy. You can train your mind as you train your body in fitness. Affirmations are powerful exercises that strengthen your mind and spirt. As you speak positive power words, you change your emotions, your aura, and the health of your physical body.

INSPIRE BODY, MIND, AND SOUL

When you give from the heart, expecting nothing back, you reap the true meaning of faith. Although you may never know the full impact of your gift, the act of giving will never come up void; it nourishes the body, mind, and soul.

Always stay true to yourself. Don't fear change. Sometimes our lives have to be completely shaken up, changed, and rearranged, to relocate us to the place we are supposed to be.

Let love guide your life, and the promise of perfect harmony will be present in all you do. Be patient, and make every effort not to let differences divide you from those you love.

We all want to know we matter. One of the greatest joys in life is really connecting with people at the heart. Nothing nourishes the soul quite the same. Show others you care about them and appreciate them.

INSPIRE BODY, MIND, AND SOUL

Surround yourself with healthy, happy, positive friends.
These friends will have an impact on your daily
behavior. Protect yourself from people who possess
negative attitudes and habits; their behavior will work
against your good intentions.

Find joy in being exactly who you are! Amazing things
happen to people when they stop worrying about
their faults and failures and embrace themselves
unconditionally. Part of a healthy lifestyle is in loving
your whole self—body, mind, and spirit.

Peace and love start with a hug, smile, or handshake.
Your attitude is your interpretation of the events of life.
Open your heart and allow love to guide you.

When you think abundance, you focus more on what
you have than on what you don't. Your perception of
happiness begins with you.

Beauty is about being comfortable in your own skin. Beauty is self-confidence; it comes from the inside. You know when someone has it. It's so much more than a dress size, lipstick, or accessories. It's that sparkle in your eye that screams *I love and respect all of me unconditionally.*

Glance at your problems, but stare at results. Don't let disappointment or pain hold you back. Any problem you have is subject to change if you really want it to change. Make up your mind that you are in control!

You are what you eat. No amount of exercise can reshape your body without proper nutrition. You will never regret the results of clean eating and daily exercise. Build your diet around fruits, vegetables, whole grains, legumes, nuts, and seeds. Make peace with living a healthy lifestyle in body, mind, and spirit.

Try a new healthy sport with a friend or as a family. It's a healthy way to bond, get your workout in, and try something new. Keep your fitness fun and competitive.

INSPIRE BODY, MIND, AND SOUL

Conjure up the highest thought you can think about yourself each morning before starting your day. Cradle it in the palm of your hand; hold it in your mind and heart. This is who you really are! Forget the rest; forget the fears of the voices from the past. You have the courage to take the next step and become who you want to be.

Freedom to think and stand on your own takes courage. Fear propels us to attach to others. Being too dependent on others isn't really living. When we hang too closely, our journey is hindered. In order to be free, we must be fully accountable for where our choices lead us in life. The key to having real happiness is taking full responsibility. Be free like a butterfly, free to fly alone. Let no one hold you back.

Words are powerful. The sound of a positive word can illuminate your path. Be mindful of the words that you say and those that you keep close to your heart.

This moment is perfect to take inventory of all your blessings. It's time to celebrate your transformation to optimism and to all your healthy habits. Just by initiating gratitude you take a big step in the right direction toward greater success.

INSPIRE BODY, MIND, AND SOUL

Meet daily challenges gracefully and with complete
confidence. Fill your mind with loving, empowering,
and nurturing thoughts. A positive mind-set goes hand
in hand with good health. Optimism is more powerful
than any muscle in your body.

Thinking positively is a healthy habit you can learn. It's
never too late to adopt a new healthy habit. Start each
day mentally acknowledging what you are grateful for.
Building a practice of gratitude is the best way to create
a healthy, joy-filled, successful life. Remember, positive
things happen to positive people.

Happiness is never about what someone or something from the outside gives to you. It is always about what you give to yourself on the inside. All the answers are within you. Simply search your soul, and let the light from within empower you to be your best.

Imagine living in ways that foster harmony rather than dissension. Strive to be nonjudgmental, and communicate with others by listening rather than convincing. Talk less, listen more, and be open-hearted. Live healthily, and be harmonious in body, mind, and soul.

INSPIRE BODY, MIND, AND SOUL

You have every right to make healthy choices. Letting go of toxic people and unhealthy relationships is not about giving up; it is about choosing your health and well-being. Make new, healthy traditions for you and your family. Stop doing the same thing out of habit. Relationships should elevate you, not drain you. How you spend your time shapes you. It creates the life you have now.

The journey to becoming who you are meant to be should be your greatest inspiration. Don't compare yourself with others. Keep striving, stretching further, and moving closer to your goal. Your path will cross those of others so that you may share lessons, compassion, hope, and grace. Appreciate and cherish each step and every encounter.

True friends are always in style. They empower the body, mind, and soul. Friendships can have a major impact on your health and well-being. Having one close friend that you can confide in can extend your life by as much as ten years. Give your best friend a hug, and celebrate life.

It's a beautiful day when you wake up and realize you're exactly where you're supposed to be. Your relationships should be based on people who add texture and quality to your life, as opposed to guilt or obligation. Spend time with people who make you happy and who are genuine. An important part of a healthy lifestyle is having healthy friendships and healthy family relationships.

INSPIRE BODY, MIND, AND SOUL

Early to bed and early to rise makes you soar with excited energy, expectancy of newness, laughter, and joy. Adequate sleep is a key part of a healthy lifestyle and can benefit your heart and brain and boost your mood. Think of sleep as the tune-up you need to run smoothly. As you sleep, your body actually repairs and restores itself. Getting enough sleep will help you significantly manage stress throughout the day. Rest easy, and let your positive energy flow.

Be patient and committed to living a healthy lifestyle. Simply remind yourself to take one day at a time. Stay on course, and trust that progress and inner awareness are all you need today. Each choice brings you closer to your goal and clears the path to healthier living.

It's time to break up with negativity today. Let go of any negative thoughts that do not make you feel strong and healthy. Retrain your mind, and put aside any unhealthy criticism. Stay focused on what you can and will do. You have the power.

Engage with the beauty of the world. Your reality is where you are right now; it's impossible to go back to yesterday, and it's impossible to predict what will happen tomorrow. Keep your thoughts engaged with your physical presence in the current moment. Breathe in only feelings worth keeping. Let go of what no longer serves your highest and best self.

INSPIRE BODY, MIND, AND SOUL

It's time to take charge of your life before it takes charge of you. We are the authors of our lives and we can write healthy new scripts that cast us as powerful, balanced, and worthy. You are what you choose to become. You are not what other people tell you you are. You are not your past. You are God charged, supercharged, power charged, and you take charge of living your life healthy in body, mind, and soul.

Letting go of a bad habit is really just creating a new habit in exchange. To create real change, you need more than just willpower. You need a plan of action. Remember that what the mind decides, the body will follow. You are not your old habits!

God is the best listener. He hears every word and feels every emotion. I will never miss an opportunity to say thank you for filling my heart with so much love for life. Be thankful for what you have, and you will find that you have so much more.

Think of exercise as a pleasure. The ability to get up and move your body is a privilege and should not be looked at as a burden or chore. Get excited about your next workout, my friends; so many people don't have the opportunity.

So many people live within unhappy circumstances and yet will not take the initiative to change their daily habits. Try something new, and discover something about yourself you didn't know. You don't have to travel the world to experience something new. Happiness is just an adventure away.

There is a vast difference between being alive and actually living. Never allow waiting to become a habit; live your dreams and take risks. If we wait until we're ready, we'll be waiting for the rest of our lives. There will always be reasons not to do something. Make a leap of faith. We are not here to play it safe.

Feel free to dream that impossible big dream. Don't listen to people who say your dreams are impossible; they say it because they gave up on their own dreams a long time ago. This is the time to make a choice and never look back. No regrets! Every moment is the right moment to work on becoming the person you want be. Chase your dreams, starting now.

Embrace new chances to grow and evolve. Be devoted to do better in every area of your life! Never stop learning. Allow life's opportunities to develop your character, and become the best possible version of you.

Always choose the high road. Allow patience, prayer, and peace to be the character- building tools that determine your approach and response to any situation that God places in your path. Every situation that is placed before you will bring you closer to your highest and best self.

To make a difference in someone's life, you just have to show how much you really care. Extraordinary things begin to happen when kindness touches someone's heart deeply. Be kind.

As often as possible, do something thrilling. When you're full of pure joy, the body produces chemicals that make you feel good all over. Feeling blissful works on both the physical and spiritual level to enhance beauty, magnify happiness, and build an enriched life. Be willing to expand your energy to experience new things and go to new places. It's so worth the effort to get out of your comfort zone.

Be proud of who you are, and don't allow others to disrupt your journey. Love who you are. Love what you are doing. Celebrate that you are not looking back with any regrets. Celebrate your journey.

Inspire Body, Mind, and Soul

Be more spontaneous. Invite more playfulness, passion, and humor into your life. Having a playful and loving philosophy toward life leads to better health and improved relationships. Channel your inner child, and go out and have some fun. Enjoying your life is part of a healthy lifestyle.

Stop stressing about what can go wrong, and start being positive about what will go right. Take control of your life, and learn to live without fear. Sometimes you just need to relax and remind yourself you are doing all you can.

Diet and exercise complement one another. A healthy diet without exercise will leave the body absent of shape and tone. Exercise without proper nutrition is counterproductive because for the body to repair itself, the nutrients and elements used have to be replaced. One is as important as the other. Remember, abs are made in the kitchen!

Broken hearts heal faster at the gym. Working out your grief will give you immediate relief. Plus, you will look fabulous! Take charge, and become the master of your mind and body. The pain will lose its hold over you. Stand on your own, and work through the pain, not around it. You're allowed to scream, you're allowed to cry, but you're never allowed to give up!

INSPIRE BODY, MIND, AND SOUL

You can speak success into your life. You are what
you think, speak, and believe. Share motivation and
inspiration. Words are powerful tools, to be used wisely;
remember, you never know who you may be inspiring.

Exercise is one of the biggest contributors to effective
personal productivity. When you exercise, you will feel
more energized and less stressed throughout the day.
The increase in happy hormones in the brain improves
your mood, relationships, and overall well-being.

Surround yourself with healthy, genuine, positive friends. Protect your spirit, value your time, and expend your energy on the good things in life. Letting go of unhealthy habits may mean detaching from negative people or a toxic relationship. You are allowed to outgrow relationships. You have every right to change your mind. Set healthy boundaries, and make your life your own.

Don't start your day in neutral. Set your mind on greatness, and be completely committed! This is the day the Lord has made. Leave any biased thoughts behind. Ignite good thoughts, and go out expecting good things to follow you today. Your thoughts determine your attitude, your actions, and ultimately your destiny. Take control of how you think, and you will be able to take control of your life.

INSPIRE BODY, MIND, AND SOUL

Learning how to laugh at yourself helps to destress any situation. Humor is a positive coping mechanism that not only improves your mood; it also builds self-esteem.

The one quality that all successful people have is the ability to take responsibility. Taking full responsibility means understanding that you cannot change all people or circumstances but you can certainly change yourself. Break the habit of making excuses or playing the blame game. The choices we make are ultimately our own responsibility. In the long run, we shape our lives, and we shape ourselves.

Today's the perfect day to let go of one unhealthy habit. Transitioning out of a bad habit can be really uncomfortable at first, but your calm and centered energy will support you and your new positive behavior. To create real change, you'll need more than just willpower; you'll need a new mind-set. Complete abstinence from a bad habit for twenty-one to thirty days will be enough to break it. You are worthy of so much goodness in your life. Make the decision to live healthfully and enjoy life to the fullest.

Achieve inner peace by focusing on positive energy, wisdom, and love. The way you view the world around you is the way you will experience it. Always look for the good in every situation. The moment you start acting like life is a blessing, it starts to feel like one.

INSPIRE BODY, MIND, AND SOUL

Motivation: when you grab hold of an idea and don't let go of it until you make it a reality. Inspiration: when an idea grabs hold of you, and you feel compelled to let that impulse or energy carry you along. You get to a point where you realize that you're no longer in charge, that there is a driving force inside you that can't be stopped. Listen to your intuitive inner voice, and find the passion that stirs your soul.

It's time to fully consider the thoughts, beliefs, and intense feelings you bring to the table when it comes to food and body. Are they positive and life-affirming? Are they fearful and judgmental? And finally, can you see the potential connection between your nutritional health and the story you tell yourself about food and body? Start feeding and telling your mind and body how powerful you are!

Be aware of the way you carry yourself. If you stand strong and tall, with your head and shoulders up, you project energy and confidence. Connect and align your body, mind, and spirit to your highest frequencies.

An ounce of gratitude goes a long way. Gratitude is a great way to express appreciation for others and boost your own happiness. Start your day with gratitude, and end it with appreciation. A simple thank-you goes a long way in bringing joy into your life from beginning to end.

Inspire Body, Mind, and Soul

Success comes to those who claim it, and it is yours to grab. Losing weight is not easy; finding time to exercise isn't easy. But making your body healthier, strong, and beautiful are rewards that are worth the effort. Affirmations help to make the connection between mind, body, and soul, which is essential for total fitness and a healthy life.

Nothing can take away your joy; you have to give it away. You're in complete control of your happiness. You become what you focus on. Make your thoughts radiant with happiness, health, and prosperity. See good outcomes, and feel them in your mind's eye. See yourself living the life you desire. Don't settle for anything less than your best!

Your words have power to start fires or quench passion. Kind words do not cost much. They never blister the tongue or lips. Kind words bring out the good nature of others and can accomplish so much. Today, start a message of kind words, and uplift a friend or a stranger. There is no telling where the good vibrations of these words may travel.

Maintaining a healthy life balance is essential for happiness and well-being. Well-balanced people have a far greater ability to focus their attention and energy on attaining their goals, taking productive actions, and moving forward in a meaningful, balanced way.

It isn't what you have, or who you are, or where you are, or what you are doing that makes you happy or unhappy. Instead, it is most likely the things you are thinking about that are altering your mood. Today, take control of your thoughts, and delete anything negative from your mind. You are in control, not your emotions. Make them empower you!

It takes great courage, strength, and maturity to hold on to your center during times of untruth and hurt. Being silent is not a sign of weakness; it is wisdom to understand that a bad reaction only fans the flame of false drama. Let love create a shield to surround and protect you. Truth can never be destroyed, just delayed.

Never give up. Take a look at whatever is going on in your life that is overpowering you. Challenge all that is no longer serving you. Declare your independence, and take your power back.

Every time you show kindness, you project positive energy. Each kind gesture helps to improve another person's mood and can make a difference in the way that person treats another, and so kindness is propelled forward. Be the leader of kindness, and change someone's day today.

Inspire Body, Mind, and Soul

Weight training is like the fountain of youth. Lifting weights builds muscle. Muscle burns more calories than fat, so the more muscle you have, the more calories you'll burn all day long, helping with weight loss. Start pumping, and stay forever young in body, mind, and soul.

Start a fitness journal, and record your success. It's the best way to challenge your mind and keep yourself accountable. Write down your goals, and then record everything you eat and drink and all the activities you do each day. Set long-term and short-term goals so there is always a time frame to work toward. It's a proven method for losing weight and improving your shape.

Start each day with a thankful heart. Remembering to be grateful daily for your health, family, and friends is the best way to start your day. You will attract an abundance of love, joy, and peace, and gain a prosperous heart to share with others.

It has been proven time and again that people who keep a fitness journal have a far better chance of success than those who do not. No matter the level of fitness, everyone can benefit from keeping a fitness journal. It can become the most rewarding part of your healthy lifestyle.

Inspire Body, Mind, and Soul

Family and friends may not always support your healthy lifestyle. Your time for exercise and effort for eating healthfully can threaten people in your life. Don't be sabotaged. This is your journey to better health. Encourage them to join you. Couples, family, and friends who train together stay together.

Take baby steps to a healthy you. Don't underestimate the power of walking. It's important to remember that no matter how badly you want to change, it will still only happen one day, one step at a time. So get walking! The fittest people I know understand the power of walking. Start today, with no excuses.

If you can walk, you can get fit. Walking gives the same benefits as traditional cardio. It's convenient for any age, anytime, anyplace, no gym, no equipment, no money—no excuses. Only two thousand extra steps a day can make the difference between being overweight and being slim. Try it, and experience the fit habit of a daily walk.

Each time you exercise, you help your body release the tension of the stress response, making you feel calmer, safer, and healthier. Certain hormones released by exercise have been shown to slow and even reverse the aging process. Getting exercise helps you build muscle, lose fat, and feel great. So why not? Exercise is a natural need of the body, just as important as the body's need for food and rest.

Inspire Body, Mind, and Soul

Start exercising, and create rejuvenating benefits. Exercise will build strength, tone muscle, and restore the appearance of youth. So look, feel, and think you are gorgeous because that's what exercise will make you.

Incremental changes determine your weight-management outcome. It's the small things you can add or change. So, make at least one small change a week. Week one, drink more water and less soda. Week two, walk thirty minutes a day. Week three, eat more fruits and vegetables and cut out unhealthy desserts. Week four, get more sleep. Week five, join a gym. All these small changes add up over time and are life-changing. One step at a time. Slow and steady wins the race. Win a long, healthy life.

Every day, respect, cherish, and honor your body. You've been given only one body, so don't take your health for granted. Take good care of your body, and live every day healthfully for you and your family.

Everyone has time for a quickie. Little quickie exercises have a big impact on your weight, your energy levels, and even your brainpower. Take just ten, fifteen, or twenty minutes to do some exercises. No excuses. You deserve to treat your body well. It needs exercise every day. Find the time!

INSPIRE BODY, MIND, AND SOUL

Sometimes your eyes are too critical, and you see what you don't want to see. That tells you it's time to start with a fresh image. Clean off the smudges and fingerprints in your mirror, and start with a sharp, clean view of life. Be a builder, not a destroyer! Start with yourself, and then pass it on and see all the beauty reflect back. Life can be so beautiful—just change your focus.

Stretching is the most neglected part of fitness. Stretch, stretch, and stretch some more. Stretching helps you become more aware of how you feel both inside and out. It's really important as we age to maintain pain-free movement in our joints. Remember to breathe. You'll feel calm and connected rather than tense and rushed.

Flexibility is crucial. When you stretch, you pump blood carrying vital nutrients to your muscles and tendons. Stretching before your workout helps to minimize your chances of injury during exercise. After you exercise, stretch to release those toxins from your muscles that build up during your workout. It may seem like a waste of time but it's a wise investment in your body. Stretching is an important part of living a healthy lifestyle.

Doing your best is a great habit to develop. It just always feels good, with no expectation of reward. The reward is how you feel inside. Today, do your best to fulfill the needs of your body, and share that powerful feeling with others.

INSPIRE BODY, MIND, AND SOUL

Accept every struggle as if it were a physical workout.
Trust the process of building your spirit. In time
you will celebrate the spiritual changes just like you
appreciate a great workout. You will feel and see the
changes and welcome them. Trust God; He has been
building spiritual giants for a long time. Celebrate and
trust the process with endurance.

Love your family unconditionally. Most people spend
their entire lives trying to fill their emptiness with
imitation love, but all they achieve is an ever-deepening
frustration. Love empowers us to live life with the
knowledge and conviction that we are here for a reason.
Love is the nourishment we need to feel secure enough
to become successful.

Discover the secret to youth when you increase your water intake. Cellular hydration is the secret to maintaining a youthful glow and overall better health. Soak your cells with water-rich foods. Water is the magic remedy that helps erase wrinkles and slows down the aging process. Don't merely drink water; you also need to eat foods that contain water, like fruits and vegetables.

There are no happier people on this planet than those who decide that they want something, define what they want, get hold of the feeling of it, and then joyously watch it unfold. That's the feeling of your hands in the clay. You are the artist creating your masterpiece. Make it as beautiful as you want.

Inspire Body, Mind, and Soul

You can have peace of mind, improved health, and an ever-increasing flow of energy. Life can be full of joy and satisfaction. Aspire to your personal greatness. Let your spirit soar. Your soul is always trying to expand. Let that true spirit shine and reach for the stars.

Visualization can transform your world to anything you desire. Whatever you want, wants you. Imagine your life exactly the way you want it to be. See it, and believe that you deserve the life you visualized. Einstein said imagination is more important than knowledge.

If you don't design your own life plan, chances are you'll fall into someone else's plan. And guess what they have planned for you? Not much! It's time to take control of your life. You know what is right for you. Make a plan today. Take one positive step toward your desired future. That is the path of no regrets!

Courage is a habit. My favorite kind of courage turns dreams into reality. This kind of courage is a vision and it refuses to be defeated. This kind of courage takes real guts. It sees. It knows. It wants. This courage will not be quieted. Make courage a daily habit. There is no challenge too big or too small.

Inspire Body, Mind, and Soul

Love always seeks to express and expand. Open your heart each day, and welcome love in your thoughts, choices, actions, and reactions. It's the only way to really live life. Peace, love, and fitness equal happiness.

Morning is the most beneficial time to exercise to burn fat and elevate your mood for the entire day. Get a partner, and commit time each morning. Your motivation will become greater each day. Make it a habit. Your life will begin to change; confidence will be your friend. Exercise is the key to greater success. Trust me—you won't wish you stayed in bed.

Stop wishing, and get determined. The difference between hoping and wishing is significant. A wish is a desire for something that seems unattainable. But nothing is impossible with God. Hope expects with confidence. Faith builds hope, knowing God wants to give you the desires of your heart. Today, actively put your determination where your desire is.

How you express your love shapes the quality of your life experiences. Strive for a fresh perspective to each new experience. Enjoy the excitement of the adventure that is your life.

Inspire Body, Mind, and Soul

Never underestimate the power of your mind. The body achieves what the mind believes. Believe it to achieve it.

A miracle can happen when someone is encouraged. Encouraging words inspire success. You are surrounded by people of all ages who need a word of encouragement. Powerful, positive words can spur amazing accomplishments.

Stop suppressing your anger. Make it work for you, not against you! Anger is a powerful emotion. When channeled properly, anger can have a positive effect. Turn your anger into an irresistible force. Find constructive ways to harness that energy and put it to work for you in a positive change. Take it to the gym!

In order to give love, you must know how to receive love. Without love, we have nothing. We all need to find that balance of a healthy body, mind, and spirit. With love, all is possible.

Today is your wake-up call. Wake up, and experience life. Wake up, and bless each morning! Appreciate friends and family. Wake up to all the love and beauty that surrounds you, before it's too late. When our minds are filled with light, there is no room for darkness. Be the light, and wake up to a beautiful life.

Practice kindness, and you start to be kind. Practice discipline, and you start to become disciplined. Practice forgiveness, and you start to become forgiving. Practice charity, and you start to become charitable. Practice gentleness, and you start to become gentle. Practice what you preach, and be the example you want to share. Actions speak louder than words!

How do you get a flat, toned tummy? Creating amazing abs is a combination of exercise and eating a very clean plant-based diet. You have to strip away the layer of fat to expose those abdominal muscles. Anyone can do this with a healthy, clean diet.

Great things take time, so be patient with yourself. Growth is a process; let go of the world's mind-set of instant gratification. If everything we wanted came easily, we would not really value or appreciate it. You are closer to your goals than you were yesterday, and that's what counts. Keep your eyes and faith on your journey.

Inspire Body, Mind, and Soul

Start being honest with yourself about everything. Be honest about what's right as well as what needs to be changed. Be honest about what you want to achieve and who you want to become. Be honest about every aspect of your life. Search your soul for the truth, so that you truly know who you are. Once you do, you'll have a better understanding of where you are now and how you got here, and you'll be better equipped to identify where you want to go and how to get there.

What we do and how we live our life affect how we age. In other words, it is important to live a healthy lifestyle, no matter your DNA. Your mind is more powerful than anything else.

Every time you subtract something negative from your life, you are making room for the new and better in your life. Don't act simply from habit. Be selective with your time and where you put your energy. Engage in healthy habits, healthy food, healthy relationships, and healthy hobbies. It may be time to clean out the closets. Expect new, healthy, and happy things in your life. Just make room for them!

What you think of yourself is much more important than what other people think of you. Only you can read your heart clearly and know your intentions behind your actions; only you know where you have been that shapes who you are, with your own special brand of fears and insecurities. You and only you can truly appreciate how brave you are each day you get up and face the world, pushing your way through the day, stepping outside your comfort zone to expand your experience. Remember, you are an awesome person.

Inspire Body, Mind, and Soul

You will never achieve what you want without being grateful for what you already have. You cannot exercise your power without gratitude and the right attitude. If the only prayer you say in your entire life is "Thank You," that is enough.

Today is a fresh start, a new beginning. Don't be held back by anything negative that happened yesterday, the day before, the week before. Learn from your past; let it inspire you to be true to who you are. Stop trying to please other people or be someone else. It's better to be an original version of yourself than an exact duplicate of someone else. Your version is better equipped to accomplish your unique plan, starting today!

It is not enough to know what you want. You must also know why you want it and what you will do once you have it. When we wish or desire something without considering the whole world around us, we are not honoring our place as a member of a larger human family: God's family. The truth is that we are all connected and must see the bigger picture. God knows your heart.

Exercise is addicting if you do it right. It's not punishment. The endorphins flow strong, making exercise feel wonderful. You should look forward to your daily workout.

Inspire Body, Mind, and Soul

You've been provided with a perfect body to house your soul. Give it the daily attention it needs. Honor that temple by eating healthy, exercising, listening to your body's needs, and treating it with dignity and love. Your body will give you back all you need to accomplish your purpose in life.

You are amazing just as you are. You are stronger than you know, more powerful than you think. You are worthier than you believe, more loved than you can ever imagine. You are passionate about making a difference, fiery when protecting those you love.

Journaling is honest. It's a wake-up call to what's really important in your life. Journaling helps reveal any negative thoughts that might be holding you back. You have feelings or thoughts you may not see until you become aware of them through writing. Writing can also help you unveil the dreams that are ready to be born within your heart and soul. Writing those daily thoughts on paper gets you one step closer to making your dreams a reality. Write it all down!

You can find the time for exercise if it's a priority in your life. It's a choice you have to keep making every day. Fitness is a journey with no exact destination. Each day can take you on a different path. Remember, different is also good. So do not get lost in excuses. Find and make the time.

Inspire Body, Mind, and Soul

Prioritize your time. Remember that you get to choose how you spend your time. People will inspire you, or they will drain you. Pick those people wisely. Positive energy equals positive results.

Prepare to give 100 percent of your mental effort to focusing on your fitness routine this week. Take a few minutes before each workout to mentally prepare yourself.

Stop comparing! Comparison isn't healthy physically, emotionally, or spiritually. Stay focused and mind your own steering wheel, your own business, and your own family. It's your race to run. Follow your own destiny. If you keep looking back or side-to-side, you will lose control of where you are headed.

The grass always looks greener on the other side. Stay on your path, and stop envying others. Someone else's path will take you off your course and will waste your time. You are exactly where you need to be today. Trust your path and have faith in yourself. Honor your journey in life.

Stop hanging on to fear, doubt, and insecurity. You are wasting precious time. This comes down to a question of self-love. Love and happiness are choices, choices that start with you first. You can consciously choose new responses to those same old fears, doubts, and insecurities. Realize that you are enough. Right now, today, as you are, you are enough. Be patient, have faith, and trust in yourself.

When you have a nagging feeling telling you it's time for a new challenge, go for it. Whether it's your workout, your job, or a life change, the same principles apply. You must have confidence, perseverance, and belief in yourself and your plan. Remember, attitude is everything when it gets tough, so refuse to throw in the towel.

No one can tell what kind of person you are simply by what you believe in, but rather by your behavior. So if you want your beliefs to have meaning, act upon them.

Trust your instincts to know when things are authentic and when they're not. Don't waste a precious minute of life if something just doesn't feel right. Stop second-guessing yourself. Your energy doesn't lie. You already know your answer.

Inspire Body, Mind, and Soul

You are not limited by your circumstances, your past, the economy, or what you have been told you can or cannot do. The sky is the limit. That means there is no limit to what you can and will accomplish. You are the only one who sets the limits for your life. Love your life, and be excited about your future. Be passionate about life.

Exercise is not just about looks. Exercise is just as much about a healthy body as it is about looking good. The body craves movement and whole foods. Having a strong and useful body often goes hand in hand with emotional self-empowerment. A healthy body, mind, and spirit are your privilege.

Sometimes we need motivation to exercise. Sometimes we need more than a personal trainer to motivate us to go to the gym and work out. Put yourself first, and trust that exercise and eating healthfully are really the best things you can do for yourself and the people you love. You should be your best motivation!

The best legacy in life is to leave footprints of love, healing, and compassion. Expect nothing in return. The world is full of silently hurting, broken people. Do something to help that will last, that feels beautiful. It's a double gift!

You have ideas, experiences, and talents and gifts that no one else has! Your gift to the world comes through sharing your unique perspective, not copying someone else's. When you compare yourself with others, you minimize what is great about you, something no one else can be. Embrace your own unique perspective. What you have to offer is spectacular. Own it!

Where would you be today if you didn't have that one person in your life who believed in you no matter what anyone said? Most people just need a boost, a push, a little encouragement. None of us reach our highest potential by ourselves. We need one another. Be that person for someone you love.

Happiness is in the small things you experience and the choices you make each day. Stop looking for the big events and feeling shortchanged daily. It's the everyday moments that will infuse your life with more happiness and joy. Look for the small gestures and quiet moments in life. A smile, a kind word, a wonderful meal, time with friends and family, good health, a great workout, helping someone, flowers, time with nature, or holding hands with someone you love.

Healthy relationships are based on trust, honesty, communication, and separate identities. You feel accepted for your true feelings and the freedom to share. Don't forget the value of being kind to those you interact with each day. Never take the people you love for granted. Invest in healthy relationships. It is critical for sustained well-being and happiness.

Inspire Body, Mind, and Soul

It's time to clean out your closet of clothes that no longer fit. Get rid of your fat clothes, redolent of negative thoughts and images that leave you feeling depressed and unmotivated. The first thing hanging in your closet should be something that makes you feel fit—like that sexy summer dress or bikini you plan on wearing on your vacation. It will remind you to stay motivated and healthy.

One thing that you can always count on in life is change. Sadness is the soul recognizing change. Change is inevitable in order to grow. Change is always good when we can look back and see how much we have learned and appreciate who we have become. Living your life to the fullest comes with its ups and downs, and it's so worth it. Joy always comes when we embrace life instead of resisting change.

Diets don't work, changing behaviors does! Develop healthy new behaviors, such as eating more nutritiously and exercising more. Make a healthy lifestyle your number-one priority. Everyday consistency is the key to success.

Laughter is good for your health. The medicine of laughter will save you money. Laugh away tension, and relieve pain. Some days you may need a good cry or a belly-hurting laugh. Both together are better! Keep a happy heart and a cheerful mind, and you will enjoy life more. Life gets heavy, so keep it light, and laugh the small stuff off. Life is about living well, loving fully, and laughing till it hurts.

Inspire Body, Mind, and Soul

A wise grandmother once said, "Good manners sometimes means simply putting up with other people's bad manners." No matter how disrespectful others may be, don't stoop to their level. Always rise above. Remain unstained and graceful.

Learn to celebrate the successes of others. Let them shine bright. Nothing is more special than seeing someone fulfill a dream or reach a goal. Nothing feels worse than the feeling of jealousy. Don't compare yourself with anyone. Your time to shine will come, and the real support of the people you love will make all the difference.

What you think, so you are and will become. Your thoughts hold the key to your future. You always get to choose. You are in control. Stay focused and determined with a loving heart.

The mind as well as the body demands daily training if it is to perform to full capacity. You can't go to the gym just once per week and walk out with a new body, and neither can you say just one prayer and expect God to make life perfect. Each day, be spiritually active, and exercise your body, mind, and soul.

INSPIRE BODY, MIND, AND SOUL

Don't hold back on love. Don't let your heart be cold. Trust that in order to receive love you must open your heart. You have nothing to fear. You are lovable and have much to share. Leave a mark of love wherever you go today. Love is a souvenir, once given never forgotten. Nothing feels better than love!

A checklist for today: (1) I followed my heart and intuition. (2) I said what I needed to say. (3) I did what I needed to do. (4) I made a difference. (5) I know what true love is. (6) I am happy and grateful. (7) I am proud of myself. (8) I became the best version of me. (9) I forgave those who hurt me. (10) I have no regrets, and I am fully living in the moment.

Never deprive someone of hope. It may be all they have. Be a dealer in hope, free of charge. The greatest gift to give someone is hope. Consult not your fears but your hopes and dreams. Think not about your frustrations, but about your unfulfilled potential. Concern yourself not with what you tried and failed in, but with what is still possible for you to do. If someone you know has lost hope, go restore it today, and you will be richly blessed.

You are not your past. No matter what emotional garbage you have, it's your responsibility now to discard it, heal it, and finally free yourself from it. No more blaming! It is possible with courage and commitment to be the happy, emotionally healthy, balanced person whom you want to be.

Inspire Body, Mind, and Soul

You are unrepeatable. There is a magic about you that is all your own. You are special and have something beautiful to share. Don't ever think what you have to give is not of value.

When you have a dream from God in your heart, you don't have to struggle to force it to happen. You don't have to be worried or frustrated, wondering if it's ever going to come to pass. When you have the promises of God deep in your heart, God is going to see you through. It's a place of faith, knowing that God is in complete control, and at the exact, right time, He will bring your dream to pass! Remember, there is no expiration date on your dreams.

Speak with vision, clarity, and kindness. Words can destroy. A spoken word can never be taken back. What you call another becomes what you think of that person and instills it in your heart and mind. Pleasant words are a honeycomb, sweet to the soul and healing to the bones.

Breathing deeply helps clarify our thoughts and feelings. It can release tears and tension. As you exhale, let go of all you would like to release. Nourish your body and soul with this exercise daily. Remember, given a stingy amount of oxygen, our bodies, hearts, and mind will not function well. So breathe down into the center of your belly. Let it go. It feels so good! Your blessings are only a breath away.

Living a healthy lifestyle should not require one to give up living a "real life." A happy lifestyle for a lifetime is the main goal. Finding the balance is individual for everyone. Start trusting and implementing each positive choice that leads you on the path you want. A healthy lifestyle is a journey, not a destination. Make it enjoyable because you will never continue doing something that you hate.

What distractions are keeping you from being and feeling your personal best? Being too busy is a distraction that we create unconsciously to avoid doing something we know we need to do. It's time to get rid of worn-out excuses. No more unnecessary distractions. It's time to make time for you. Your name should be first on your schedule. Feeling and looking your personal best will benefit every area of your life. You will never regret investing in yourself.

The two most important days of your life are the day you were born and the day you discover the purpose for your being here. Live life purposefully! Live life passionately! Live life blissfully or you're just not living the life you were put here to live. Start living life today.

It doesn't matter if you're a child or an adult; the people you spend time with influence the person you will eventually become. The people you associate with can elevate you as much as they can bring you down. Be selective, and pay attention to the company you keep. Be around supportive, loving, positive people, such as friends who want only the best for you. If your presence doesn't add value to their lives, their absence will make no difference in yours.

Inspire Body, Mind, and Soul

Stop waiting to be happy. Stop waiting for that calculated time. It will never be perfect. Being happy doesn't mean that everything is perfect; it means you've decided to look beyond the imperfections. Life is full of imperfections. See the joy and beauty in all of them. They're all gifts; they just come in different sizes with colorful bows.

Healthy self-esteem stems from internally held positive beliefs about yourself; not from the approval of others. Focus your attention on your own character instead of what others may say, do, or feel. Save that precious energy for a healthy, positive you.

You will never know how important your willingness to reach out to others may be, or how one hug can totally change an otherwise difficult or lonely existence. Start in your own home, by hugging your friends and family every day. A touch of a hand or a warm hug is good for your health and heart. Start hugging!

When you follow the dream in your heart, you are fueling your life for beauty. Like a flower needs water, your dream needs sunshine. Live your life to the fullest; it's contagious and will attract others to feel the same. Be confident that God may be sending you that special person to help accomplish your dream.

Inspire Body, Mind, and Soul

Exercise is to the body as a raindrop is to a flower. Refreshing, invigorating, life- changing. Do not even imagine a day without some form of exercise. Your body craves movement.

The foods you put in your body will make you either healthier or ill in the long run. Eat for longevity. Only plant foods contain healing energy. Look at meals as an opportunity to refuel and energize your body with whole, healthy, nutritiously satisfying foods.

Happiness is like a butterfly. The more you chase it, the more it will elude you. But, if you turn your attention to other things, the butterfly will come and sit upon your shoulder. May the perfect one, at the perfect time, come to you.

Your future has a special purpose that only you can fulfill. You are capable and worthy to accomplish what has been placed in your heart, so let nothing hold you back. Walk completely secure; no more delays, you really got this.

Appreciation makes people feel more important than almost anything you can give them. Remember, your true friends appreciate you for who you really are. Flaws and all, unique and one of a kind, there's no need to try to be somebody else. You are always good enough!

Eyes filled with love look through a telescope but eyes filled with envy look through a microscope. When feeling critical about someone's flaws, convert those feelings into ones of love and appreciation. You may be surprised at how quickly you can change your perception.

All of us need attitude adjustments at times. When negativity takes hold, it's time to convert that energy into positive thinking. You've probably heard the saying "your attitude determines your altitude." Choose to fly high and keep soaring. Remember, attitude is the little thing that makes a big difference.

When dining out with friends and coworkers, don't be tempted to follow the usual unhealthy, overeating, and overdrinking crowd. Be a leader. It sends a message that you take care of yourself responsibly and effectively. Successful people show a pattern of behavior that is respected in all areas of life. It could benefit your career and make you stand out. Be different; being different is good!

Inspire Body, Mind, and Soul

Are you looking for a habit that will help you reach a ripe old age with little effort? An afternoon nap can help you live longer. An afternoon nap is the secret to the fabulously high age reached by the oldest inhabitants of the island of Ikaria. Napping, by encouraging you to relax, reduces blood pressure. Along with a healthy diet and daily exercise, you will not age as quickly as those who don't nap.

Faith tells me that, no matter what lies ahead of me, God is already there. Fitness prepares me for the journey of life and helps me live life completely. The benefits of a healthy lifestyle are far beyond physical. Being healthy in body, mind, and soul keeps me balanced, strong, disciplined, motivated, and committed.

This is your life, so do more of what makes you happy and makes you smile. Life is meant to be vibrant, deeply felt, and fully engaged. Use your time wisely, and enjoy some fun while you make lasting memories that time cannot erase.

Let go of any fear, any doubt that holds you back from the life you really desire. Decide today to commit to your life! No more excuses, no more regrets. Be ready, willing, and able to make a mature commitment to your life.

Inspire Body, Mind, and Soul

There's always another level to reach in your healthy lifestyle. It's important to have goals and challenges to keep yourself motivated. You can keep getting healthier, stronger, and younger. Weight training will make you feel amazing.

Your happiness in life is directly related to your depth of your gratitude. You can retrain your feelings and attitude with a grateful heart. Love expresses gratitude. A grateful person can find contentment regardless of his or her circumstances. Part of a healthy lifestyle is sincere gratitude for the life God has given you and the privilege to start the day with exercise.

Getting older is inevitable but aging is optional. Your body is your temple; so don't fuel it with junk. Love, respect, and nourish all of you. Remember, you are loved.

Throughout your life there will be people who will criticize you. People may judge you, and some may try to belittle your ambition. They may feel threatened by your accomplishments. Keep company with people who uplift, love, and support your healthy lifestyle. God will allow opportunities that will encourage you, and goal-oriented people like yourself will come into your life.

Inspire Body, Mind, and Soul

The best goal you could ever have is to know God better. Faith reflects inner courage, and hope has only positive expectations. I have learned you don't have to keep looking over your shoulder because God always has your back.

The whole world is waiting for you…it's time to step up! Everyone wants his or her life to count for something, to be meaningful, and to make a difference. True significance is found in following your higher purpose and loving others. If you want your life to have meaning, then give of your heart, and look for ways that you can help serve other people.

Sometimes it takes moving farther away from something to see it for what it really is. A different view can give you a whole different perspective. Maybe today all you need is a little distance to help see things as they really are.

It's time to really show up for your life! Anything worth achieving is worth working for. Wishing for something to happen is different than working toward making it happen. To achieve any goal, you need a strong faith, discipline, and perseverance. With courage in your heart, take a stand, take a deep breath, and begin to design the life you want to live. It's time to take action and make some progress.

Inspire Body, Mind, and Soul

Let go of what doesn't make you happy. Be present, be free, and laugh as much as you can. Start enjoying your life today. Remember, nothing is owed to you, and tomorrow isn't guaranteed.

Create healthy choices, not restrictions, for yourself and your family. Buy a variety of healthy foods to cook together. Suggest fun, healthy activities for everyone to participate in. Make living a healthy lifestyle something they get excited about. It's their decision; let them arrive at it, their way. You and your family will never continue doing something that you hate.

Set yourself up for success with a variety of healthy foods in your home. I always have a variety of healthy options in all food groups. Failing to plan ahead can lead to unhealthy choices. You and your body deserve quality, nutritious food. Plan ahead, and make your food in advance. Always make the healthiest choice possible. This is living a healthy lifestyle.

People can correct or heal only what they are ready to acknowledge, accept, and let go of. The best way to build a new life is to depart from your old ways. Separation of unhealthy habits is the only way to break free. Let go of toxic food, toxic relationships, and any negative habits that no longer serve your highest and best self.

Fun is necessary! It delivers oxygen to the soul. If you've lost that fun feeling, it's time to get it back. Fun is about living in the moment and a willingness to be open to it. It's about being spontaneous. Fun, joy, and excitement should be part of your healthy lifestyle!

Sometimes what you're searching for comes to you when you least expect it. God knows what's in your heart. Never lose hope or faith. Remember, God's timing is always perfect, and so is His love for you.

Vision looks through the chaos of the moment to what is beyond, in the context of the big picture. What vision or desired goal are you holding onto? Make a commitment in writing even if this means looking ahead at the impossible but believing in your dreams. Affirm it now!

The benefits of laughter are similar to a mini-workout and actually offer some of the same advantages of exercise. Laughter offers a sense of joy, bringing peace and balance to your life. Take a mini-vacation throughout your day; laugh and smile more. It's good medicine for the body, mind, and soul.

Inspire Body, Mind, and Soul

Be happy because it's good for a healthy body, mind, and soul. A positive attitude and a joyous spirit give you the strength to be your best. Happiness is a choice to be embraced daily.

Set your intentions for the week ahead. People who have a healthy mind-set achieve. Believe you are worthy of all the goodness and abundance God has in store for you.

Remember, you are beautiful, intelligent, creative, guided, and brave. Now go after what you want. Having the right attitude makes all the difference.

The friends we meet along the way are those we are destined to meet. People come into our lives for some reason, though we don't always know what it is. Even pets and other animals that we come in contact with play some kind of role in our lives. Some may stay for a lifetime, while others may only stay for a short time. Each and every experience with another soul teaches us something about our own.

Inspire Body, Mind, and Soul

People will give advice and insights on how to live life, but when it comes down to it, you must always do what feels right for you. Always follow your heart, and, most importantly, never have any regrets along this amazing journey of life.

Don't get lost in yesterday. Today is more of a gift than you realize. Your biggest blessing may be that unanswered prayer. God wanted you exactly where you are today. Keep moving forward in faith to experience your true miracle. Close your eyes, and feel that promise. It's closer than you think. God is always faithful.

Life is all about choices. It's never a one-size-fits-all. Many times we find ourselves making choices to fit in with people and places where we really don't belong. Instant gratification usually involves regrets. Be selective with your choices. Don't compromise the perfect fit for you.

Fun is a big motivational factor when exercising. If you associate your workouts with excitement, exercise will become an enjoyable part of your lifestyle. If you hate exercise, you will never be able to make it a habit that you can stick to. Remember to mix up your workouts, keep that body guessing, and try something new and challenging. Start having fun with your fitness, and make that a part of your healthy lifestyle.

Inspire Body, Mind, and Soul

Exercise your willpower to be your best. Willpower is like a muscle: the more you use it, the stronger it will get. This week, pick one healthy habit that will make your life better. Commit everything in your power to make it happen. By making consecutive, healthy lifestyle choices, you will build your self-esteem and remain in a strong positive mind-set. You can accomplish anything you put your mind to. The more you exercise your willpower, the easier it will become.

Change is good. Transformation is a necessary step to growing stronger and wiser to get where you want to be. Are you aiming high, digging deep, conquering challenges big and small to build the body and life you want? You must push yourself daily out of your comfort zone. Most people play it safe because they secretly fear change. Each day, strive for progress, not perfection. Make one positive change in your life today that will get you closer to where you want to be.

Self-confidence is your best accessory. Self-confidence is sexy and attractive. Be passionate about your health, and honor your body, mind, and spirit. Practicing discipline and taking good care of your health will boost your self-esteem and give you the confidence to achieve your dreams.

Wake up this morning, and smile. Smile from the inside out. Connect all of you in perfect harmony to use what talents you possess to serve your higher purpose. You have so much to share. Don't hold back any part of you. When you give everything and expect nothing in return, only then will you be in a position to gain everything.

Inspire Body, Mind, and Soul

Believe in the sun even when it's not shining. Believe in the power of the human spirit. Believe in love even when you don't feel it. Believe in life—that we are all here to fulfill a special purpose. Believe in God even when He is silent. Believe that words of grace filled with love touch and nourish our body, mind, and soul.

Think of the good people who have helped you thrive. Like healthy food nourishes the body, when you interact with good people, that good will multiply with you. You will gain knowledge, new skills, wisdom, understanding, and appreciation.

Always keep the focus on the positive, and try not to let one bad experience allow you to forget the power of goodness. Let your gratitude multiply on to others. Share love, light, and a kind, generous heart; that is something we all seek. God is good all the time.

Today is the day to recommit, refocus, and rebelieve in the power of positive change. You can change anything you desire. "Born this way" is not a valid excuse. People can change. Goals can change. You can start changing your life today with one bold, brave, healthy new habit. It takes a touch of genius, a lot of courage, and a bit of class to move in the opposite direction.

Laughing makes you feel alive, connected, and beautiful. Laughter is very important for the human body. It is a powerful antidote to stress, pain, and conflict. Laughter lightens your burdens, inspires hope, connects you to others, and truly has the power to heal and renew. Your sense of humor is one of the most powerful tools you have to foster your daily mood, emotional state, and good health. We all need more laughter in our lives.

What's your favorite cardiovascular activity? Everyone should aim for at least thirty minutes of exercise at least five days a week. Cardiovascular exercise includes any activity in which you move your large muscle groups for a sustained period while maintaining an increased heart rate. In addition to burning body fat, cardio activities help condition your heart and lungs to move blood and oxygen throughout the body more effectively. Practice a heart-healthy lifestyle!

When you truly value your body, mind, and soul, you will find peace within yourself. Part of living a healthy lifestyle is being able to free yourself from comparison, rejection, and the control of others. When we depend on the approval of others to feel good about ourselves, it's impossible to have emotional stability or a healthy self-image. Letting go allows you to live in balance and harmony.

Live life courageously. Draw a line in the sand for those forces that hold you back from achieving your desired goals. Don't stay focused on disappointments or failures. Look at these as lessons to better achieve victories and success today. It's all in how you train your mind. No experience is ever wasted. Focus on God's grace for today. You are healthy, strong-willed, strong-minded, and able to conquer life with a positive mind-set. It's time to go get what you want!

Inspire Body, Mind, and Soul

Your opinion of yourself is more important than other people's opinions of you. Your truth, discipline, and courage will define who you are. Being confident in who you are will become your daily habit.

Your words are a powerful antidote to stay encouraged, motivated, and nurtured. Delete any negative or fearful thoughts that enter your mind. Expect to rise above any negativity. Stay positive, focused, and encouraged with your life-affirming thoughts and words. What the mind decides, the body follows.

When you wake up today, take a moment to reflect on all the goodness and beauty in your life. A beautiful day begins with a healthy mind-set. Focus on the positive. It is truly a privilege to be alive and healthy. Take nothing for granted, for it is all a gift, and nothing is guaranteed, not even tomorrow. Do something healthy and different today to bring you closer to the life you want to live.

Trust your intuition; your soul wants you to make decisions. When you choose to listen to your heart, it's like a beautiful dance without knowing all the steps. It's a natural flow like the wind—you are expressing who you are.

Visualization is accomplished through concentration, focus, intention, and repetition. Successful athletes use this technique all the time. Improve your fitness with visualization. Find your focus, stay with it, and build on it. Where the mind goes, the body follows. Visualize each body part, and imagine each muscle at work. Imagine you surpassing your goals and becoming stronger with every workout.

Start your day with positive affirmations. Use your own words to motivate yourself. Tell yourself you are getting stronger, leaner, healthier. Affirmations ready the mind for success. Make it your daily exercise, and practice to expect greatness.

Every time you respect and release your emotions, you are healing a part of yourself. Never apologize for your tears. Crying is the only way your eyes speak when your mouth can't explain. Your tears cleanse your soul in order to move forward. All these feelings need to be felt. Suppressing tears and emotions increases stress levels, contributing to diseases such as high blood pressure, heart problems, and ulcers. Release and let go so you can get back to smiling.

You cannot change your destination if you don't make a move. Thinking but not acting will not get you any closer to where you want to be. You can change your direction if you have gotten off course. A shift in your thinking and a step in a different direction are all that may be required. Try not to overthink it; baby steps will still get you where you want to be. Slow and steady wins the race. God has not given us a spirit of fear and timidity, but of power, love, and self-discipline.

Certain people pretend compassion and concern. They will assure you how much they care, understand, and relate to your personal situation; they may even claim love for you and to have your back always. When the true moment comes for demonstration of understanding, what you may get is misrepresentation, abandonment, insensitivity, or rejection. Don't let that experience close your heart to other people.

Every experience can be a blessing if we learn from it. Be devoted to putting forth the effort and energy required to gain clarity at the beginning of all relationships. Unless we take time to gain clarity in the beginning, we may find ourselves in the company of experienced imposters.

Understand that no one can hold you back from your life's mission unless you allow it. Stop giving away your power. This is the defining moment—when you realize it's really up to you and you need to stop allowing anyone to interfere. It takes courage, faith, discipline, and consistency to follow your life's calling. With the right heart, the right people, the right actions, and an unwavering passion, greatness will prevail.

Today, run the extra mile, dig deep, and find your inner strength. Find ways to help share the burden of other people until they are strong enough to stand on their own.

Inspire Body, Mind, and Soul

Focus on filling your mind and time on things that are true, noble, reputable, authentic, compelling, and gracious. Never settle for anything less. You are worthy of greatness.

The key to living a healthy lifestyle is commitment and consistency. Stop vacillating, and truly make it your lifestyle. Choose love over fear. When you're able to stop compromising your truth and operate from a place of love, you take full responsibility for yourself, and that's when your life changes.

The time has come to shine some light and energy into creating the things you wish existed in your life. Your attraction will draw your desires closer to you. See it in your mind's eye, visualize it over and over again, become what you respect. Mirror healthy habits that you admire and deserve in your life. The time is now to put a plan in action and really start living your truth.

Looking for an all-natural way to boost your mood? Turn to Mother Nature. Sometimes just soaking up some sunshine, breathing a little fresh air, and feeling your toes in the grass can provide relief from stress, anxiety, or depression. Being outdoors can be a healthy mood booster. Couple the effects of exercise with the mood-boosting properties of the great outdoors, and you'll address your body's physical and emotional needs.

Inspire Body, Mind, and Soul

What if you woke up today and you simply said, "Thank you, God"? I promise it will be a joyful day. You are blessed and loved. Open your heart to God's grace and love for you.

Be grateful. Sometimes what you think you want the most you're better off without. Stop agonizing over what you think you want, and be grateful for what you have.

We have a choice each morning to use the gift of life to make the world a better place or not bother at all by staying fixed and rigid. Life holds so many possibilities when you have an open mind and a loving spirit. Stay true to your path, and you will surely find the treasure you seek. The best part is making many new friends along the journey.

You can't wait for inspiration to get your workout on. Some days you just have to go out and be your own inspiration. No excuses; put on some great music, and make your own circuit. You just may inspire yourself and someone else.

Inspire Body, Mind, and Soul

The simple act of smiling can change a person's day.
A kind gesture or appreciative words can change a
person's life. Be generous with your affection, and
extend kindness. There is no danger of kindness
running out; your kind ways will return to you tenfold.

Run from gossip, whether it pertains to an enemy or
a friend. Your participation in any gossip will only
bring negative energy to your body, mind, and soul.
Remember what it feels like when someone hurts
you with gossip. Rise above low energy with love and
kindness by not participating in gossip.

Take time for a little TLC after a long day. Your body will honor you when you honor it. Treat your body as a treasure, worthy of respect, and it will respond in kind. Your body is your vehicle for life. You must love, respect, honor, cherish, and treat it well. There are no trade-ins. Neglect and abuse of your body can have serious consequences.

Give yourself permission to laugh. You'll be amazed how quickly something that looks or feels like a crisis can turn into a comedy when you allow a little humor into your life. Laugh it off, and try not to be so serious. It's so important for all of us to learn to laugh at ourselves. Having a sense of humor can be a lifesaver.

Inspire Body, Mind, and Soul

Laughter causes stress to vanish. There's a very good chance that what you're angry or upset about today you won't even remember a year from now. Laughter teaches you to lighten up and take yourself less seriously even in the most serious situations. Sometimes, it can help you gain a better perspective in the complexity of life.

Mental health is just as important as physical health. Looking good on the outside is something we all desire but feeling healthy on the inside is so much more important. Don't exchange one for the other. Honor each part of yourself; seek balance, not perfection. Everything works in your favor when you love and accept your true self.

Is it time for a new chapter in your life? Maybe it's time to tell yourself a new story in order to shift your mood and spirit forward. Rather than waste your energy on negative emotions, channel it into something more productive. Make it powerful, successful, and beautiful.

Ride your own wave. Don't compare your life to anyone else's life. When you trust your own unique flow of ups and downs, you will find a more peaceful existence.

Inspire Body, Mind, and Soul

Your perception of life and the decision to think positively are your keys to good health and abundant happiness in your life. Positive energy attracts more of the same.

It feels so good to listen to your heart. Trust not that events will unfold exactly as you want, but that you will always be fine. You will reach a new level of happiness by understanding that your current situation didn't happen to you; it happened for you. Trust every step of your journey.

When you wake up every morning, think what a privilege it is to be healthy, to breathe in life, to eat, to enjoy and love people and the things that we take for granted. Try to cultivate more gratitude and happiness in your thoughts. Choose positive thoughts over negative thoughts. Make it a beautiful day.

Music can be a powerful tonic to affect your mood. When working out, listening to music will enhance your focus and create an intense desire to work harder. Choose music that allows you to connect to your power, your magnificence, and your true potential.

Inspire Body, Mind, and Soul

Finding a few minutes throughout your day just to do nothing is healthy for you. The sounds of nature, the wind, birds singing, or the soothing sound of water can be very healing, transforming, and nourishing to the body, mind, and soul.

Never allow anyone to make you feel insignificant. Who you are and what you have to share matters. Your life is a precious gift—do not allow the opinions of others to impact the course of your life. Instead of trying to please others, work on being satisfied with who you are. Not everyone is going to like you. Accept it, move forward, and use your positive energy to live your best life. The most important relationships are the ones that you have with God and yourself.

Inhale and welcome new challenges. Stay true to yourself. It's better for people to respect you for who you truly are, not for who you pretend to be. It takes more courage to express your truth. Don't be afraid to be yourself even if it means removing yourself from lives that don't nourish or value you.

Don't suck up your feelings. Suppressing true feelings is the worst example to give a child and very unhealthy for the adult who does so. Repressed feelings will eventually manifest into unhealthy habits. You are worthy of love, respect, and being valued. So are your feelings.

Inspire Body, Mind, and Soul

You are the master of your own happiness. Happiness is not what happens to us but how we choose to live our lives. How many times have you said, "I'll be happy when—I'm thinner, richer, or more successful"? If your happiness is due to circumstances, you will never be satisfied. We have little or no control of life events but we do have control over how we respond. Make happiness an intentional activity.

Make a list of things that make you feel joyful, and let it remind you which activities to engage in when life throws you a curve ball. Whether exploring nature, meditating, exercising, cooking, playing sports, or simply spending time with people you love, choose activities that lift and empower you. Attitude is everything, and you are in control.

Why are you here? What's important to you? What is your life truly about? Stop sacrificing your core values. Don't make excuses; don't compromise—if you believe good health and exercise are important, stop putting off what you need to do today. Align your goals and actions in order to live a happy, healthy, fulfilled life.

Without a vision you are without a future destination. Those without a vision spend their lives taking the path of least resistance to avoid discomfort or fear of failure. The level of sacrifice that a vision requires will measure the determination and willpower of the people who follow through. Have a clear vision of how you want to live your life.

Inspire Body, Mind, and Soul

He who hesitates is lost. Stop putting off what you know deep in your heart you need to do today. Take that one step to improve your health. No act is too small to get you on track. Just start! Not only will this enable you to live your best life but your healthy lifestyle will empower you to become a greater influence on everything and everybody around you.

How do you exercise healthy control as part of your success story? Effort is the word that comes to my mind. When you find yourself daydreaming about where you want to be, you also need to visualize the effort required to get to that point. The reality is that willpower, optimism, and hope require one thing: your continuous effort. Make it your goal to do everything you can do actively and inwardly to bring yourself closer to where you want to be. If you talk the talk, you must walk the walk.

Now…today…this very moment…you can choose to change your thinking. Make the choice on a daily basis, preferably first thing in the morning, to think loving, healthy thoughts that make you feel powerful. Affirmations are like seeds planted in soil. Poor soil, poor growth. Rich soil, abundant growth. Remember, every empowering thought, healthy choice, and action matters.

Hugging is good for your health. It transfers energy and gives the person hugged an emotional lift. Some say you need four hugs a day for survival, eight hugs for maintenance, and twelve for growth! Scientists even say hugging is good medicine. Ten seconds of hugging can lower your blood pressure. Hugging therapy is a powerful way of healing: it restores the mind, body, and soul. A hug can make any situation better. Nobody ever regrets a hug.

Inspire Body, Mind, and Soul

To achieve maximum health, build strength. Weight training is the fountain of youth. Get under some weights and lift. Variety is key.

Once you achieve a major goal, you will not be the same person you were when you started. The process of achieving your goal and the experience you have gained will forever change you. The journey is just as much the reward as the goal. Nothing compares with your earning something you have worked for. No matter how much wealth you attain, you can't buy character; that's an inside job.

Many of us have something we are holding onto that we need to release to become healthy in body, mind, and soul. The measure of your maturity is how spiritual you become in the midst of your frustrations. Weak people seek revenge. Strong people choose to forgive. My healthy friends like to exercise. Spiritual people pray and trust God will work His way.

The mind is the master of the body. If we train and discipline the mind, the body will follow. Allow only positive thoughts to enter your mind today. Positive thoughts are the fuel for the body-mind connection while exercising. Negative words are the fuel for failure. What the mind decides, the body will follow. You have the power to decide what kind of workout you will have even before you start.

Don't use your energy to worry; use your energy to believe. Renew your mind every morning. It's a new day to get excited and expect miracles. God loves to turn impossibilities into realities. A miracle is the way God supports you, reminds you of your importance, and of His creation in your life. You are worthy of miracles. Go ahead, ask, believe, and you will receive.

Are you all in or not? Stop with the halfhearted effort; nothing halfhearted will never fulfill your wholehearted desire. If we are halfhearted in our pursuits, we can only get halfway. Go all the way! Let go of the fear holding you back. Wholehearted effort is where you want to be, that's what brings on real results. Get fully committed, and watch the magic happen!

It's good to set healthy boundaries. Move beyond any doubts that you can share your truth in a healthy, loving, positive way.

Open your heart to seeking healing, wholeness, and God's supernatural love. God has so much He wants to bless you with. You may not only experience miracles but also learn to expect them daily. Appreciate the blessing of friends who can walk, talk, and celebrate miracles with you. God always shows up in our lives. Keep your heart open to His love and blessings. Expect that your miracle is on its way. It's going to be an amazing day.

Inspire Body, Mind, and Soul

Exercise and diet alone will not give you the body that you desire. Your mind must be equally engaged to reach the goals that you set forth. The same is true for your soul. It is important to your overall health that your mind, body, and soul work together in sync to give you the focus, strength, and empowerment that you need.

Silence is golden. Turn down the noise and listen. Taking time to meditate each day is just as important as a healthy diet and exercise.

Fitness is not easy; if it were easy, everyone would achieve it. It's a desire to have a strong body and mind. Believe in yourself and all that you are. Bring out your inner force, and crush all obstacles. Strive for progress to give or do more. Perfection is not required. Just do your best.

Set fitness goals, and reward yourself when you succeed. Give yourself full permission to recognize your achievements. Be your own champion.

Inspire Body, Mind, and Soul

It is really true that happiness is a result of what you believe and what you do, not a result of what happens to you. If you understand this, you can have a happy life. There is a season for everything. Sometimes bad things have to happen before good things can come to pass. Keeping this in mind will help you to live a happier life.

Never take abundant health for granted. You must do your part with time and discipline to stay healthy. Never undervalue your health and how precious a gift it is to you. When you have your health, you have everything. When you do not have your health, nothing else seems to matter.

Begin each day with gratitude. Live each day having the courage to be vulnerable, living life fully, honestly, with no regrets. You will attract all the qualities you display.

Live your life to the fullest. Focus on health, energy, and excitement. Eat to live, don't live to eat. Make sure to enjoy every bite. Envision success. It all starts in your mind. Decide to unlock the power to feel healthy and happy.

Inspire Body, Mind, and Soul

Healthy anger gives people the momentum to produce necessary change. It can give you the power to leave a bad situation. It can motivate you to start eating healthier and working harder. Healthy anger can be constructive in making a difference in your life forever. If you are living unhealthily, it's time to get angry enough to make the change once and for all.

Exercise not only offers physical rewards; exercise provides emotional, spiritual, and financial benefits as well. Poor health can be very expensive. Make a healthy lifestyle your number-one priority. It will bring balance into every area of your life…body, mind, and spirit.

The greatest gift that you can give to another person is your time. Not just when it's convenient, but when you spend time selflessly with someone in need. The times when someone needs you the most are usually not the times most convenient for you. It is through these opportunities that your actions speak louder than words.

Make mercy a part of your healthy lifestyle. Start today! Healthy and good relationships are impossible unless we are generous with mercy and forgiveness. Good relationships grow stronger when we learn to give and receive forgiveness.

Inspire Body, Mind, and Soul

The kind of person you are determines what kind of life you attract. When you feel good, you attract and manifest even more good. What's going on at the heart of the matter really tells your life story.

Let your life be filled with joy. Exercise helps to radiate joy from the inside out. Joy is so attractive. Seek your own joy, not the world's view of joy but your very own. Allow yourself to sparkle and shine. Sharing your joy is the greatest gift that you can give to anyone.

Today's soul exercise is to expand your values and discover that the good life doesn't just depend on good circumstances. True happiness is the result of what you believe and what you do, not the result of what happens to you. No matter what life throws at you day to day, you can rise above it all and know God's love is greater than the worst of days. Choose to refuse bitterness, even in hard times.

Do you realize how important getting enough rest is for your body, mind, and soul? To lose weight, three simple rules need to be followed: eat a clean plant-based diet, exercise regularly, and get plenty of sleep. While the first two rules of losing weight are obvious to everyone, few people pay attention to the third step—sleep.

Inspire Body, Mind, and Soul

Some people get their only exercise by jumping to conclusions, running down friends, side-stepping responsibility and pushing their luck. Choose to be different; choose to be better than the rest!

When you stop chasing the wrong things, you give the right things a chance to catch you. Stop focusing on things you don't want to happen. Use your energy wisely to fully begin making the changes that will really matter in your life now and tomorrow. Change your mind, and the rest will follow.

Self-confidence comes from really knowing who you are. Embracing your own uniqueness, delighting in your one-of-a kind ways, feeling satisfied with your individual self! A lot of people forget that their individuality is what makes them so special. Self-confidence is sexy; own it and love it!

Today's exercise is a mental shift to lighten up and let go of taking everything so seriously. Your frustration level is largely of your own creation; it's composed of the way you want, see, and expect your day to unfold. No day is problem-free, but your attitude and reactions can be. Adapt to the flow of life as if taking part in a dance. You might miss a few steps but you can still enjoy the music.

Inspire Body, Mind, and Soul

Don't give up the fight to be fit and healthy. This is where your choices matter most! Learn the balance of a healthy lifestyle with clean eating and daily exercise. Don't throw in the towel and waste all your hard work and discipline. This is when it really counts. Decide right now: "I will reach my goal, and nothing will stop me. I have the power and discipline to make it happen!"

Good relationships, good health, and being good at what you do all require some sacrifice, discipline, discomfort, and some pain. How many times do we ask for what we want and expect it without putting in some effort or work to get it? Take full responsibility for everything in your life, and get the results you really want. No more regrets, no more settling for less than you want and deserve!

The key to a healthy relationship with food is to look at it as nourishment for a healthy body, mind, and soul, not as a crutch or reward or entertainment. The fact is that eating is something you need to do several times a day. Take the fear and deprivation out of eating, and find your healthy balance. Make peace with food.

What's in front of you is much more powerful than what's behind you. Stay on track, and don't look back. You have all the power to create a new you, along with new habits, new choices, a new mind-set, and a new weight. It's time to find a new beat, a natural rhythm to your life. Make healthy the dance of your life, moving, stepping to a new groove.

Inspire Body, Mind, and Soul

When you reach for a higher level of success, your friends and family may have a hard time letting go of the old you, but resist the pressure to return to your old self. Your future is a higher level of newness to a healthier you. Be a leader, not a follower.

The energy that you put forth into the world will return to you. The law of reaping and sowing is the most powerful force. People who sow healthy lifestyles reap good health, and those whose lifestyles are unhealthy reap sickness. Stop hoping against hope, and begin living healthfully. Be mindful of what you eat and how much you exercise. Choose a healthy diet and daily workouts. You will reap positive results in your health; it's really as simple as that.

Do you have healthy friendships? If you're wondering if one of your friendships has become toxic, ask yourself if the friend feels dishonest even a little and takes way too much effort. If the friend is overly critical, much too negative, and feels like toxic energy. If the friendship is one-sided and disrespectful. If you are outgrowing that person. If so, life will be happier, calmer, and better without him or her. Consider whether you're staying in the friendship out of choice or out of obligation. Only you know the answer for yourself.

The truth is that people change. Life events, stress, age, and time all have an impact on how we see the world. Sometimes new values and goals disconnect us from old relationships. Life is about changing and growing, but we all move at a different pace. Sometimes the change in one person works to motivate another. Other times the change wedges the friendships apart. Realize when it's time to let go of old relationships in order to reach your full potential.

Inspire Body, Mind, and Soul

Goals should be specific, measurable, attainable, realistic, and timely. A specific goal has a much greater chance of being accomplished than a general goal. To set a specific goal you must answer these six questions: Who is involved? What do I want to accomplish? Where do I need to go? When do I need to be there? What are the requirements and constraints? Why do I want to do this? Remember, it's never too late to start working on your goal.

Be brave, follow your heart, and don't regret the dreams left unexplored! Have courage, trust in yourself, and keep moving forward.

Don't quit just because you didn't meet your original expectations. Stop expecting perfection. Think progress, not perfection. Trying to achieve perfection is too much of a burden and will set you up for disappointment. Perfection is a goal that will always be out of your reach. No person, place, or thing is perfect except God. Each day, with God's help and steady improvement, you will move closer to your dream. See it, believe it, and achieve your personal best one day and one prayer at a time.

Choose the thoughts you put in your mind just as you choose the food you put in your mouth. Let healthy thoughts nourish your mind as healthy food does for the body. You are in control, so dismiss any unhealthy thought that makes you feel bad. Nourish your mind, body, and soul with every thought and bite today.

Inspire Body, Mind, and Soul

Love recognizes no barriers. It jumps hurdles, casts out all fear, and sets you free. May you be forever full of hope, strength, and a strong will. Never stop believing how powerful you really are. Surround yourself with people who appreciate you, lift you up, and remind you of all that you have to offer. Let go of anything or anyone who no longer belongs in your life. Be healthy in body, mind, and soul.

INDEX

Abundance 6,44
Acceptance 23,81,93,95,153,155
Accountability 2,21,29,30,55,65,128,
    147,177,181
Achievement 163,168
Adventure 57
Affection 162
Affirmations 16,19,37,40,47,48,63,
    108,109,122,131,143,146,162
Anger 88,171
Appreciation 7,15,24,25,36,42,48,74,
    78,119,151,152,170
Aspirations 101,123,179
Attitude 2,120,131,132,155,159,176
Attraction 1,148,173

Balance 4,12,24,27,41,55,70,113,121,
    130,153,171
Beauty 45
Beginning 35
Being Different 13
Belief 137
Breathing 112

Challenges 3,4,10,20,22,49,94
Change 14,30,55,66,77,79,105,119,
    135,138,144,154,171,175,180
Character 36,58,59,115
Charity 172
Choices 40,99,127,134,150,175
Clarity 126,145

Commitment 147
Communication 42
Compassion 102
Confidence 3,14,45,60,68,99,118,122,
    125,133,136,141,154,166,175,176
Consistency 5,20
Control 1,12,24,26,38,40,45,55,
    61,71,98
Courage 47,71,84,126,138,140,146,181
Crying 144

Destiny 51
Determination 160,181
Diet 1,2,9,14,17,28,38,46,62,67,68,
    90,106,117,120,124,128,167,170,
    174,178
Discipline 33,34,136,144,146,147,
    169,177
Diversity 13
Dreams 58,111,116,181

Effort 161,165
Emotions 38,144,158
Empathy 7,151
Empowerment 1-3,7,8,9,13,16,19,
    20,26,32,43,47,49,54,72,87,92,93,
    100,120,124,126,132-134,140,141,
    144,146,154,157,161,162,164,167,
    175,180,183
Encouragement 11,15,44,72,87,95,
    107,110,111,141

Endurance 36

Envy 98

Excellence 37

Exercise 1,2,5,9,10,12,14,16,29,37,39,
46,56,62,63,68,73,75-80,85,88,90,
94,96,101,102,117,123,134,139,
150,156,163,164,167,168,171,173,
174,179

Expressions 86

Faith 3,12,14,22,41,56,86,111,121,
125,129,133,137,149,155,
165,166,174

Fear 23

Feelings 158

Fitness 5

Fitness 3,9,10,12,13,18,20,39,46,
53,62,67,73-76,78,90,95-97,
101,121,127,134,139,143,150,
163,168,171,177,179

Focus 2,3,15,17,25,26,55,97,
98,113,138,140,142,147,
170,175,177

Forgiveness 34,164,172

Friendship 25,33,35,39,43,52,
119,132,180

Fun 18,129,134

Generosity 41

Goal Setting 1,2,5,8,10,11,13,20,27,
28,31,58,64,66,73,74,77,80,82,
84,91,92,94,96,105,113,130,135,
138,146,148,160,163,165,168,
177,178,180,181

God 3,12,14,22,41,56,86,111,121,125,
129,133,137,149,155,165,166,174

Gossip 15,151

Grace 49

Gratitude 22,48,49,56,68,74,
93,123,142,149,156,170

Grievances 16

Growth 58,105

Guilt 6

Happiness 4,5,18,21,25,30,31-34,
38,41,43,44,47,50,57,60,69,71,
82,99,104,106,113,115,118,122,
123,127,129-131,133,136,148,
153,155,159-160,169,174

Harmony 42,50,13,140

Hate 15

Health 1,16,21,53,63,67,82,91,95,
113,124,128,140,148,152,166,
169,171,174,177,179

Honesty 1, 91

Hope 86,110,125,129,183

Hugging 116,162

Humility 7

Humor 139

Hydration 82

Inspiration 56,67,101,116

Intention 33,131

Intuition 8,31,142

Journaling 73,74,96,130

Joy 4,38,42,43,60,61,69,83,
115,127,129-131,159,173

INSPIRE BODY, MIND, AND SOUL

Judging 23

Kindness 15,18,59,70,72,89,112,116,151,

Laughter 65,106,130,139,152,153
Leadership 179
Learning 14
Letting Go 19
Listening 7,50
Losing Weight 68,77,106,120,128,
174,178
Love 12,15,17,23,32,42,44,78,81,
85,86,88,89,103,104,109,119,
125,132,183

Meditation 8,30,167
Mental Health 153
Mercy 172
Miracles 22,165,166
Motivation 2,36,37,51,56,57,67,72,
79,96,102,105,143,150,171
Music 156

Nature 107
Nurture 37
Nutrition 9,14,16,28,40,67,117,
128,178

Opportunities 58
Optimism 6,49
Oxygen 112

Passion 3,114
Patience 2,27,42,53,90

Peace 12,44,66
Perception 155
Perfection 182
Perseverance 126,182
Persistence 20,34
Perspective 126
Positive Thinking 4,6,8-10,13,20,
23,24,26,29,30,34,35,40,45,
47-49,54,55,61,63,64,66,71,83,
87,91,92,98,106-109,115,119,
120,135,138,141,147,154,
156,162,164,167,169,175,176,
178,182
Prayer 30
Pride 60
Privilege 156
Procrastination 7, 161
Progress 182
Purpose 41,114,118,125,160

Relationships 51,52,59,64,71,75,81,
86,89,97,103,104,107,112,114,
116,124,127,128,132,137,145,
155,157,158,172,180,183
Respect 2,7,21,32,36,37,78
Responsibility 55,65,177
Rest 53,121,174

Self-Esteem 1,8,13,16,19,22,38,
65,95,103,110,111,115,152,157
Self-Improvement 89,92
Self-Love 8,31,37
Self-Pity 3,6
Sharing 21,33,104,138,172

187

Silence 167
Sleep 16,53,121
Spirituality 164
Spontaneity 61,129
Stamina 4
Starting Over 7,35
Stress Management 6
Success 10
Support 33,39

Time Management 14,15,97
Transformation 135
Trust 8,100,111,154,155
Truth 16,17,19,91,166

Understanding 23
Uniqueness 103,110

Vision 130,160
Visualization 11,26,28,31,83,97,
143,148,161

Water 82
Weight Lifting 163
Weight Loss 27
Weight Management 68,77,106,
120,128,174,178
Willpower 9,135
Worry 6,165

Made in the USA
Lexington, KY
03 July 2017